The Red Poppy: Josef Stalin at Home

A Dramatization of Yuri Krotkov's *The Red Monarch*

The Red Poppy: Josef Stalin at Home

A Dramatization of Yuri Krotkov's *The Red Monarch*

J. Ajlouny

PUSH PULL PRESS
GUNTERSVILLE

THE RED POPPY: JOSEF STALIN AT HOME
A Dramatization of Yuri Krotkov's
The Red Monarch

Copyright © 2018, 1999, 1998
by J. Ajlouny
All rights reserved

Push Pull Press
An Imprint of:
Fresh Ink Group, LLC
Box 931
Guntersville, AL 35976
Email: info@FreshInkGroup.com
FreshInkGroup.com

Edition 1.0	1998
Edition 1.1	1999
Edition 2.0	2018

Digital Stalin painting by Anik / Cover by Geez
Book design by Amit Dey

Many of these essays first appeared in a variety of publications including *Novosti Today, Soviet Life, The Detroit News, The London Observer, Spy, The Utne Reader* and other newspapers and magazines.

Performance: Any performance of this play must be licensed in writing by the publisher, including royalty arrangements. No alterations, deletions, or substitutions of a material nature may be made in this work without prior written permission of Fresh Ink Group, LLC. Authorship credit must appear on all programs and promotions in all media where space permits.

Publication: Except as permitted under the U.S. Copyright Act of 1976, no part of this publication may be reproduced, distributed, or transmitted in any form or by any means, or stored in a database or retrieval system, without prior written permission of Fresh Ink Group, LLC.

BISAC Subject Headings:
DRA016000 **DRAMA** / Russian & Former Soviet Union
PER011000 **PERFORMING ARTS** / Theater / General
PER020000 **PERFORMING ARTS** / Monologues & Scenes

Library of Congress Control Number: 2018948535

ISBN-13: 978-1-947867-21-5 Papercover
ISBN-13: 978-1-947867-22-2 Hardcover
ISBN-13: 978-1-936442-82-9 Ebooks

Prologue

In darkest night, cold and clear
The earth turns its sleeping head.
Widows and children shiver in fright,
Seeking refuge beneath the martial bed.
Dusk to dawn, uncertain hours
Have ever been the pleasure of evil minds
No church bells toll anymore
Only a single spotlight shines
And who is caught in that beam
We called friend just yesterday
Nothing changed that we could see
Except the chains he wears today.
But soon the sun will shine and restore the light of man's desire.
Soon the ground will ignite and burn us all in eternal fire.
When, from the ashes others rise
As others always must
The deeds of the past will never die
Nor memories turn to dust.

—J.A.

The Red Poppy: Josef Stalin at Home

Based on: *The Red Monarch* by Yuri Krotkov

Medium: A seven scene play in two acts. Approximate performance time 105 minutes plus one intermission.

The Time: The Autumn of 1949

The Place: Stalin's dacha Bluzhnaya, forty miles outside of Moscow.

Setting: The parlor of Stalin's dacha is a large stately room filled with book shelves, papers, clippings, newspapers, magazines, etc., neatly stacked throughout. There are characteristic photos of Marx and Lenin on the wall. Two adjacent sofas fan-out at center stage with a table between them; a conference table is at stage right. There are three doors at rear stage left, one which leads downstairs, one which leads to Stalin's private study and one to his bedroom. See stage design floor plan.

Synopsis: The play seeks to translate *Krotkov's* serious and satirical image of Stalin onto the stage. The overriding theme is the elusive, sometimes delimiting quality of power, a phenomenon, that even an absolute dictator such as Stalin is forced to recognize.

Also portrayed are the chief members of Stalin's personal entourage, his right hand man Beria, the ruthless KGB chief; his secretary, his housekeeper, his bodyguard, his Politburo colleagues and others equally as colorful. The play is at once funny, sad, surreal and poignant. The action is packed with irony and revelation. Divided into seven separate vignettes, each scene stands separate from the rest, connected only by Stalin's overbearing strength and immodesty and his anticipation of his first face to face meeting with Mao Tse-tung, which took place in December 1949.

The author, Yuri Krotkov was born in Russia but moved to Soviet Georgia as a young boy in 1934. His father was a graduate of a Moscow engineering institute who was assigned to an electric plant in Tiblisi. Though he grew up as a member of the new Soviet intelligentsia, he could not bear the censorship and dishonor that confronted his serious writer's passion. In 1963, while traveling as a member of a filmmakers' delegation, he requested and obtained political asylum in Great Britain. He eventually settled in California and published The Red Monarch in 1978. He died in 1988 at the age of 69.

Characters in Order of Appearance

J.V. Stalin: General Secretary of the C.C.C.P.

Major P. A. Shoposhnikov: Stalin's bodyguard

L.P. Beria: Minister of State Security

Comrade Proskrebyshev: Stalin's personal secretary

Alan Brown: American journalist from Boston

N.S. Khruschev: Politburo member, Party Secretary

K.Y. Vorishilov: Politburo member, Marshall of the U.S.S.R.

A. I. Mikoyan: Politburo member, Party Secretary

G. M. Malenkov: Politburo member, Government Minister

V. M. Molotov: Politburo member, Government Minister

Rodianovna: Stalin's housekeeper and cook

Gelovani: Famous actor who portrayed Stalin on stage and screen

Sergo: Early revolutionary friend of Stalin

Sopha: Sergo's wife

Comrade Lee: Chairman Mao's translator

Mao Tse-tung: Leader of Chinese Communist party

This play requires a minimum of nine male roles and one female role. If a production cannot sustain such a large cast, the playwright suggests eliminating Act 1 Scene Three. This will obviate the need for the roles of all the Politburo members.

Prop List

- Set furniture and furnishings according to stage plot on following page.
- Men's felt slippers
- Basket of soaps and bath oils
- Men's black boots
- Portfolio of record albums
- Chinese style hand fan
- Gift box containing a traditional multi-colored Cossack dance costume
- Gift box containing a traditional bright yellow Chinese peasant costume, sash and hat
- Telephone, tea service, notebooks, desk accessories

The Red Poppy
Josef Stalin at Home

ACT I
Scene One

SCENE: Stalin's Parlor

TIME: Morning

AT RISE: A big man in a military uniform is keeping guard outside the bedroom door where he thinks Stalin is sleeping. The guard is sitting on a stool, fighting to stay awake. He is wearing slippers on his feet. Stalin, unwashed and disheveled, wearing only a long shirt and socks, enters from his private study, not the bedroom.

Stalin:
You've got yourself into a pickle again, eh Comrade Shoposhnikov? *(Shoposhnikov startled, jumps at attention.)* Ah, but you guard your leader poorly. Only last night, who was on duty, Papatov? I slept downstairs in the den and there he was—guarding the library. What a fool!

Major Shoposhnikov:
Josef Vissarionovich, how can anyone keep up with you? A bed is prepared for you in every room, but which you choose, nobody knows.

Stalin:

That's right major, nobody knows and nobody should know. Do you know why nobody knows where Comrade Stalin will sleep?

Major Shoposhnikov:

No Comrade Stalin, no.

Stalin:

You idiot! It's a state secret that's why. Nobody must know! But you Comrade Major, you are a member of the Committee for State Security. You are a captain of the internal guard. You must know! That is your duty. And, I might add, a distinguished duty.

Major Shoposhnikov:

Yes, Josef Vissarionovich.

Stalin:

The Soviet people have entrusted you with the life of Comrade Stalin. The Soviet people are counting on you major, is that not true?

Major Shoposhnikov:

Yes, Comrade Stalin, exactly.

Stalin:

And only the Soviet people?

Major Shoposhnikov:

No, the entire progressive world!

Stalin:

Shhh, not so loud. That's right Comrade Major, you remember that. The entire progressive world is counting on you. Do not, I repeat, do not let them down.

Major Shoposhnikov:

Of course, Josef Vissarionovich. I will not. My duty is as sacred as my mother to me, no, more so, as sacred as my honor.

Stalin:

Okay major, don't fall apart. Forget your mother, forget your honor. Just remember what you've learned here and I promise I won't inform Comrade Beria.

Stalin washes up in a basin and puts on his customary tunic.

Stalin:

Tell me Comrade Major, you were on vacation, where did you go?

Major Shoposhnikov:

Oh, thank you Josef Vissarionovich. We had a most excellent time at the ministry's sanatorium in Sochi. The Black Sea is as beautiful as the winter. My son, he's just ten years old, he loved every minute. Marching, hymns, socialist instruction, young pioneer indoctrination. He enjoyed himself most of all.

Stalin:
Ten years old, huh?

Major Shoposhnikov:
Yes, Josef Vissarionovich, and he loves Comrade Stalin so much. He's young, but he understands everything as if he's already had a political education.

Stalin:
Good, then you'll take him one of my books. I'll autograph it for him.

Major Shoposhnikov:
Josef Vissarionovich, that would be as wondrous as party membership to a boy so small. And of course he hates Americans, like fierce animals he does. Why, I heard him say just yesterday, "You know Papa, I would like to chop Truman's head off." *(He becomes emotion-laden.)*

Stalin:
Comrade Major, you are a war hero. You are a former boxing champion. But you're

a sentimentalist too. Did you cry after you punched your opponents in the nose?

Major Shoposhnikov:

Forgive me, Josef, it is just I love my young son so much.

Stalin:

Enough, major, I have a long day ahead of me. *(Stalin pours himself a cup of tea, then laughs loudly.)* Hey Shoposhnikov, what's that on your feet, slippers?

Major Shoposhnikov:

They are night shoes from Leningrad. My wife Seraphine bought them for me for my birthday.

Stalin:

Huh, let me see them. Take them off. *(Shoposhnikov hands slippers to Stalin.)* Not bad quality, very nice. These are... slippers... Comrade Major. We should commend the factory responsible for their production. *(Returns the slippers to Shoposhnikov.)* You have a very considerate little wife, Comrade Major. That's good, very good. A wife must, indeed, absolutely must, show consideration for her husband.

Major Shoposhnikov:
Yes, she is a treasure, Seraphine. When she gave me these night shoes...

Stalin:
(Interrupting) They're slippers, Shoposhnikov, slippers.

Major Shoposhnikov:
...She said, "Wear these in good health as you guard Comrade Stalin. They are so soft that Comrade Stalin won't hear you when you walk up to him as he sleeps to cover him or fix his pillow." So thoughtful my Seraphine and they fit me perfectly.

Stalin:
You have a very clever wife, Shoposhnikov. Tell me, what did she have in mind when she bought you these slippers?

Major Shoposhnikov:
Just as I have said. Josef Vissarionovich, so that I would not disturb you.

Stalin:
So then, you can walk up to a man in his sleep wearing your new slippers and kill him without him ever suspecting it.

Major Shoposhnikov:

Yes, …No, no, of course not, Comrade Stalin. Besides, they're not slippers, they're night shoes. Slippers have no backs; these are definitely night shoes.

Stalin:

No Comrade Shoposhnikov, they are slippers. If I say they are slippers, then that's what they are. Do you understand? I am the son of a shoemaker from Georgia. I know the difference between night shoes and slippers. These, Shoposhinkov, are definitely slippers.

Major Shoposhnikov:

Slippers, yes Josef Vissarionovich.

Stalin:

Let's perform a little experiment. I'll lie down on the sofa and you go over there and tiptoe toward me and then lean over me, as if you were going to cut my throat.

Major Shoposhnikov:

But Comrade Stalin, I…I…I…

Stalin:

Do as I say Major, go over there! *(Shoposhnikov frets, but follows Stalin's order. Stalin lays on his back and closes his eyes.)* Okay, I'm ready, start coming. *(Shoposhnikov tiptoes toward Stalin and bends over him until the two men's eyes meet.)* Again, Shoposhnikov, do it again!

Major Shoposhnikov:
Please, Josef Vissarionovich. *(Stalin glares at him and points to the other side of the room. Shoposhnikov again tiptoes to the prostrate Stalin, but this time with the addition of a slight patter. Stalin rises and points at Shoposhnikov.)*

Stalin:
Do you know what class struggle means, Comrade Shoposhnikov? It means we must be vigilant, always vigilant against enemies of our revolution. We are ants, Shoposhnikov, only ant laborers in our struggle to build a socialist state. No one, not even my bodyguards are exempt from security precautions.

Major Shoposhnikov:
But...

Stalin:
(Shouting) Silence! Do you know how many letters we receive at the Kremlin every day from people threatening to kill Comrade Stalin? *(Shoposhnikov is too stunned to reply.)* The exact

number is a state secret, but I'll tell you that it is not so few. These people threaten to break my nose, skin my hide, "My Georgian hide," or even kill me...Yes, kill Comrade Stalin. Your Stalin. They threaten to poison my food, to put a bomb in my shorts.

Major Shoposhnikov:
It can't be true!

Stalin:
One I remember most vividly. This scoundrel said he would put me in a meat grinder, head to toe. Then he said he'd fry up some patties and feed them to his apartment manager because he is a member of the Communist Party. Imagine that, Shoposhnikov, frying Comrade Stalin patties, and probably not in butter, but in lard.

Major Shoposhnikov:
Hanging such a person is too good!

Stalin:
Yes, Shoposhnikov, you are right. But back to the slippers. You now understand me, Major. The enemy is so vile and their hatred for the leader of progressive thinking is so cruel that no weapon can be ruled out, not even slippers. *(Stalin dangles the slippers in front of Shapsh's eyes*

and then picks up the telephone on the table between the sofas.) Comrade Proskrebyshev, it is I. Tell Marshall Beria I want to see him at once. *(He hangs up and turns to Shoposhnikov.)* Now go downstairs and surrender yourself to Colonel Litvinenko until Beria arrives.

Major Shoposhnikov:
I don't understand, Comrade, what do you mean?

Stalin:
You understand perfectly well, Major. Tell me, Shoposhnikov, have you ever read *Macbeth*?

Major Shoposhnikov:
No, I don't think so. But my Seraphine, she's read everything. She's a student of literature.

Stalin:
Is that so?

Major Shoposhnikov:
Yes, and her imagination is very colorful.

Stalin:
I'll bet it is. Tell me, is she fond of novels about suspense and intrigue?

Major Shoposhnikov:
Indeed, she is, Comrade Stalin. Indeed, she is. You know everything.

Stalin:
No, but I know enough. Now do as I say, surrender yourself downstairs.

Major Shoposhnikov:
But Josef Vissarionovich, what is wrong?

Stalin:
Do it!

Shoposhnikov's eyes fill with sadness. He turns toward the door, takes a step and then turns once again to Stalin, who is pointing toward the downstairs door.

Shoposhnikov EXITS with a salute. Stalin puts the slippers out of sight. Stalin lights his pipe and reads a newspaper with his feet upon the table. Beria, a short bald man with glasses ENTERS, wearing a civilian suit.

Stalin:
Ah, Beria, you're just the one I wanted to see. All is not well in our internal guard.

Beria:
Josef Vissarionovich, Bitano*, whatever do you mean? Why is Major Shoposhnikov under arrest? What has happened?

* Bitano is the Georgian word for Master.

Stalin:

Quit asking questions, Beria. I will tell you all. Then it shall be your duty to ensure that it does not happen again! *(Stalin retrieves the slippers and dangles them in front of Beria's nose.)* What do you see, Beria?

Beria:

Night shoes, Bitano, a nice new pair of night shoes.

Stalin:

(Loudly) Idiot! Slippers, Beria, these are slippers, do you understand?

Beria:

Yes, Josef Vissarionovich. I didn't look at them carefully enough, of course. A nice new pair of slippers—made of felt, I think.

Stalin:

Right Beria, exactly, felt slippers. They are felt slippers! Do you know how they got here, Comrade Minister of State Security? *(Beria shakes his head in silence.)* You know, you must know! Stalin's Minister of State Security must know everything.

Beria:

Of course, Josef Vissarionovich, and we try very hard. You know this Comrade. We have made great strides against class enemies.

Stalin:

Let the liquidation continue Beria, for we have enemies in our midst.

Beria:

No Comrade Stalin, not that fat Cossack housekeeper we sent over?

Stalin:

No Beria, not her. But now that you mention it, I hate the way she stares at me. Get rid of her, today!

Beria:

Yes, Bitano.

Stalin:

Now there is a suggestion that one of my bodyguards planned to sneak up to me in my sleep and cut my throat. I want you to tell me whose idea this was.

Beria:

It can't be, Josef Vissarionovich... *(Suddenly realizing and pointing downstairs.)* Shoposhnikov? Oh no, not Major Shoposhnikov. He's a puppy, a big baby puppy. He could have never...

Stalin:

(Interrupting) Luckily I caught him before his dreadful crime. A Macbeth he is, a fascist

capitalist Macbeth. And his wife, ah she is clever, more clever than even Lady Macbeth.

Beria:

I don't understand, Bitano.

Stalin:

I repeat, whose idea was it, Beria?

Beria:

Josef Vissarionovich, Shoposhnikov? No, it is not possible. *(Beria raises his hand to his mouth, suddenly realizing that he has contradicted the leader.)*

Stalin:

Whose idea was it, Comrade Minister? *(Raising his voice.)* The British or the Jews?

Beria:

The British, Comrade Stalin, it was definitely the British. We suspected this just the other day. It's definitely the British who were behind this plot.

Stalin:

Churchill, just what I thought. The old killer Churchill. Get Shoposhnikov up here. I want you personally to take his confession. *(Beria rings the phone and inaudibly orders Shoposhnikov to be brought to them. Shoposhnikov ENTERS disarmed, de-medaled and in shackles.)* Ah, Shoposhnikov, come in. Sit down! Talk with Comrade Beria while I have my breakfast. Be sure to listen to what he says.

Major Shoposhnikov:
Of course, Josef Vissarionovich.

Stalin EXITS, via his study door.

Beria:
You idiot! How could you be so foolish? You know he's a paranoid maniac.

Major Shoposhnikov:
What? But I didn't do anything!

Beria:
You did plenty. You know he's obsessed with finding class enemies. He is a psychopath. How could you be so stupid?

Major Shoposhnikov:
Comrade Beria, what are you saying?

Beria:
I'm saying you're as good as dead, Major! The leader himself has decided you are a British agent sent to assassinate him in his sleep.

You're finished now, Shoposhnikov, finished. How does it feel to be condemned?

Major Shoposhnikov:
It isn't true! It isn't true! Lavrenti Pavlovovich, you must save me! Comrade Stalin is mistaken, you know that.

Beria:
Mistaken? Comrade Stalin's mistaken? You tell him that, Shoposhnikov, and you'll be hanged before you're shot. The fact is, the leader is never mistaken. He proclaims truth. Stalin's truth is for the good of the revolution. We might not like it, Shoposhnikov, but we are just mice to him and sooner or later he'll eat us all. The old fart.

Major Shoposhnikov:
But I love Comrade Stalin.

Beria:
Shut up and do as I say. *(Beria sits down to think.)* Where were you born?

Major Shoposhnikov:
In Altai.

Beria:
Was your father a landowner?

Major Shoposhnikov:
No, he was a peasant farmer. My grandfather owned a moss swamp.

Beria:
Have you ever been outside the country: During the war you were in Berlin, right?

Major Shoposhnikov:
Yes, Comrade Minister and I was awarded the Order of the Red Banner for courage in battle.

Beria:
(Thinking to himself.) Fool, there were British in Berlin. Okay, Shoposhnikov, here, I will dictate your confession. Write exactly what I say and be neat about it.

Major Shoposhnikov:
A confession? No please, Lavrenti Pavlovovich, not a confession!

Beria:
Be quiet you fool! Comrade Stalin needs your confession as his proof of the valiant work he is doing in the name of the Soviet people. That's the way it is, Major. Period!

Major Shoposhnikov:
But I would die for Comrade Stalin.

Beria:
Good, here's your chance. Now write! *(Beria dictates.)* "To the minister of Internal Affairs and State Security. I confess that after the period of collectivization of farms, when my father was dispossessed as a kulak in Altai and sent to a labor camp in the Northeast, I bore a grudge against Soviet power and swore to avenge myself on account of my dead father." *(Shoposhnikov jumps up pleading.)*

Major Shoposhnikov:
Lavrenti Pavlovovich, I can't. It's not true.

Beria:
Did I say it was true? Sit down and continue or I'll have you dragged out here in chains. Don't worry, I'll handle everything. *(Beria continues dictating.)* "When I was in Berlin during the Great Patriotic War, specifically in November 1945, I came into contact with a British Agent who offered me money and western goods for my family, I received the code name Lancelot. It was my assignment to gain access to the First Directorate of State Security as Stalin's

bodyguard. My mission as received last week from the British Embassy in Moscow—from Captain Smith—make that Captain Cook, was to stab Comrade Stalin in his sleep. Signed Major Peter Alexandrovich Shoposhnikov." Now sign it, Shoposhnikov!

Major Shoposhnikov:

I can't, Comrade Beria. Think of my wife and young son. They'll be disgraced, thrown out of their apartment and ridiculed by the masses. *(Shoposhnikov begins to weep.)*

Beria:

Hold yourself together, Shoposhnikov. Do you think I would betray one of my own? Beria rewards loyalty, Shoposhnikov. Do as I say and sign the confession. I will have you transferred to a far-away republic. Kazakistan maybe. Don't worry. Stalin will never know. *(Handing Shoposhnikov the pen.)* Now sign it, fool!

Major Shoposhnikov:

(Crying.) It's not fair. All my life I've been a communist, a party member since 1938. I love Comrade Stalin with all my heart. I killed Germans with my bare hands for him!

Beria:

And he thanks you for it. You think tears will help you, Major Shoposhnikov? *(Pause.)* If you love Stalin, sign this confession, now! *(Babbling and shaking, Shoposhnikov signs the confession. Beria then grabs and examines it.)* Long live the great Stalin!

Major Shoposhnikov:

Long live the great Stalin. *(He bows his head, raises his hands over his head and starts to shake.)*

Beria picks up the phone. He is inaudible, but points his hand at Shoposhnikov and just before he hangs up, he pulls his finger past his throat.

Beria:

They are waiting for you downstairs, go now and don't say a word to anyone, is that clear? *(Shoposhnikov rises, wipes the tears from his eyes, straightens up and he EXITS.)* That old maniac! *(Beria paces around the room.)* What a lunatic, an absolute lunatic.

Stalin the RE-ENTERS.

Stalin:

I'll hand it to you, Beria.

Beria:

(Startled and horrified at the thought that Stalin was listening behind the door.) Oh, Bitano, were you listening in?

Stalin:

I heard parts of it. *(Beria cringes and falls into a chair thinking he is lost.)* Good work, Comrade Minister. No one other than me of course, is better at unmasking class enemies. Congratulations. *(Beria, relieved, rises. Stalin pins an invisible medal on Beria's chest.)* Tomorrow, we will inform the Council of Ministers that you are now a Hero of the State of the Soviet Union. *(Stalin offers his hand and shakes, then embraces him.)*

Beria:

Thank you Bitano, I am most grateful for the confidence you have placed in me. Here is the full confession, Josef Vissarionovich. We know everything.

Stalin:

(Reading the paper.) Yes, he is a scoundrel, I sensed it. He's weak, Beria, very weak. What did you do with him? No, never mind, let him be on your conscience. But one thing, he has a son. Make arrangements for him at the best

military school. He will be a fine Soviet officer. We communists are not avengers, eh Beria. Here a son does not have to pay for the crimes of his father.

Beria:

Of course not, Josef Vissarionovich, Bitano.

Stalin:

Okay, let's change the subject. What's new today?

Beria:

Nothing Bitano, everything is fine. Plans for Mao's arrival are being finalized. We are looking forward to constructive meetings with our Chinese comrades.

Stalin:

Good, we must make a good impression, Beria. Mao is a great leader. Besides the whole world will be watching us.

Beria:

That reminds me, Bitano. The Foreign Ministry is encountering great difficulty in arranging accommodations for Mao's large entourage. They have suggested we assign them an officers' barracks in the Pelatnavov Garrison and house the VIPs in the Hotel Metropole. What is your opinion?

Stalin:

Under no circumstance are our visitors to be inconvenienced. If your ministry sees to appropriate security concerns, I will not object to this arrangement. Just keep our boys away from any young Chinese women!

Beria:

Yes, Bitano, I understand. You think of everything. Tell me Bitano, you don't look well, are you feeling okay, dear Soso?

Stalin:

It's that bloodsucker Shoposhnikov. Can you imagine if he killed both me *and* Mao? The world would indeed become dark.

Beria:

We were onto him Bitano, I have disciplined Litvenenko and his men for not discovering the night shoes, I mean slippers, the slippers earlier. This was unforgivable. General Vlascek will hear about this breach of duty. It will not go unpunished.

Stalin:

Good Beria, I know that in the end, I can rely on you. You're wicked Beria, that's why I like you. Compassion is a good thing Beria, but like everything else, it has its time and place. *(It is Stalin who gets up and walks around the room.)*

Beria:

I only do my duty as you instruct me. It's not easy work!

Stalin:

And you're very good at what you do, most of the time! It's not easy being hard, I know. But it is necessary, Beria. Changing the world is never easy work. But see, tomorrow you will have your medal and the honorarium. You are highly rewarded for your toils, difficult as they may be. Go now Beria, see to Mao's visit.

Beria:

Good day, Bitano.

Stalin:

And one last thing Beria. Send a telegram to Churchill. Tell him his agent Lancelot has fallen.

Beria:

He has slipped on his own slippers. *(Stalin laughs, Beria joins in. Stalin shows him to the door and escorts him out and closes the door after shaking Beria's hand.)*

Stalin:

(To the audience.) A dog, good people, deserves a dog's death.

He returns to his reading the confession as lights go down.

End of Scene One

ACT 1

Scene Two

SCENE: Stalin's Parlor

TIME: Mid-morning, the same day

AT RISE: Stalin is sitting on a sofa struggling to put on a new pair of boots. Finally, he succeeds in getting them on. He tries them out by walking around the room. He growls in pain and returns to the sofa. Comrade Proskrebyshev, Stalin's personal secretary, ENTERS.

Proskrebyshev:
(Looking at his wristwatch.) Good day, Comrade Stalin.

Stalin:
What do you want, eh?

Proskrebyshev:
The American reporter is waiting to see you.

Stalin:
Oh, not today Proskrebyshev, send him away. These boots are killing me!

Proskrebyshev:
But we rescheduled two times already, Comrade Stalin and he is leaving Moscow tonight.

Stalin:

(Looking straight at Proskrebyshev.) You're a pain in the ass, Comrade. Okay, show him in. *(Proskrebyshev nods approvingly and then opens the downstairs door and escorts Alan Brown into the parlor and introduces him to Stalin.)*

Proskrebyshev:

Josef Vissarionovich, this is Mr. Alan Brown, the American correspondent.

Stalin:

(Shakes his hand.) The American correspondent or the American spy?

Brown:

Hold on there, sir.

Stalin:

Relax, Mr. Brown. I don't care if you are a spy. You have exactly ten minutes. But first, Comrade Brown, tell us something about yourself and please, sit down.

Brown:

Thank you, may I call you Comrade Stalin?

Stalin:

As you wish. May I call you Yankee?

Brown:

I'm from Boston actually…, never mind. Well really, I'm a rather ordinary American. I'm married and have five children, one of which wants to enter the U.S. Foreign Service.

Stalin:

Very good, make sure he learns Russian.

Brown:

I'll tell him you said that, thank you sir.

Stalin:

Okay then, let's begin.

Brown:

First sir, I have a present for you. *(Brown pulls two bottles from his briefcase and hands them to Stalin.)* These are for you. My brother and I manufacture them in our plant in Massachusetts.

Stalin:

What is it, gasoline bombs?

Brown:

No Comrade Stalin, shampoo for the hair and bath oil for the skin.

Stalin:

Oh, very good. How clever, eh Proskrebyshev? We can talk further, Mr. Brown. Products like these are in short supply in our country. We were hit badly in the war and while we have made great strides, much needs to be accomplished. Luxuries like these are, unfortunately, not priorities. Comrade Stalin thanks Mr. Brown for his thoughtfulness. Now, shall we begin?

Brown:

Okay, do you believe in God?

Stalin:

No, I am an atheist.

Brown:

Do you believe in communism?

Stalin:

Of course, I am a Bolshevik.

Brown:

How much money do you have tucked away in Switzerland?

Stalin:

Not one kopek.

Brown:

Are you planning to export your revolution to the United States?

Stalin:

No.

Brown:

(Taken aback.) No?

Stalin:

No, you have your own communists. They will make a revolution of their own.

Brown:

Why did you purge so many of your old comrades?

Stalin:

Because it was necessary for the good of the country.

Brown:

Have you ever killed anyone yourself?

Stalin:

I am the leader, not the assassin.

Brown:

Are you the author of the Soviet Constitution? The so called, "Stalin Constitution"?

Stalin:

No.

Brown:
Then who is?

Stalin:
The masses, of course.

Brown:
Ah, well put, Uncle Joe. Tell me, are you afraid of death?

Stalin:
No.

Brown:
Why not?

Stalin:
Because all over the world, people say that Comrade Stalin is immortal.

Brown:
Congratulations, Uncle Joe, your answers are irrefutable. If only American politicians were as direct as you.

Stalin:
Too bad, I'm not an American politician. I'd show them something!

Brown:
Who killed Trotsky?

Stalin:

Trotsky who?

Brown:

(Brown quickly changes the subject.) Do you consider yourself a Czar of Russia?

Stalin:

Don't be foolish. Of course not. I am Comrade Stalin. General Secretary of the Central Committee of the Communist Party of the Soviet Union. I am merely an official who happens to be the top official. Tell be Brown, how is it that you are recording my answers without writing? Do you have a secret microphone or something? That CIA of yours is very clever.

Brown:

No, I am writing your responses. It's shorthand, that's all.

Stalin:

Shorthand, what's that?

Brown:

It is a way of writing long things in an abbreviated manner. It saves a lot of time and effort.

Stalin:

Very interesting this shorthand. Proskrebyshev, note shorthand as a subject I'd like to discuss further. *(To Brown.)* But please, continue.

Brown:

You know, during the war, Americans referred to you affectionately as "Uncle Joe." How did you feel about that?

Stalin:

I was rather touched. What do they call me now?

Brown:

Well, in view of the difficulties our two countries have been experiencing since then, the fact that you have apparently stolen the plans to our hydrogen bomb...

Stalin:

What are you talking about? Are you accusing me of being a thief?

Brown:

No, of course not, but your own foreign minister as much as admitted it.

Stalin:

Can I help it if dedicated "American Communists" choose to dump secret documents off at our embassies? Let me remind you that devotion is a higher ideal than patriotism. *(To Proskrebyshev.)* That's good Proskrebyshev, make sure you write that down.

Proskrebyshev:

Yes, Comrade Stalin.

Brown:

I see. Tell me, why do you encourage the glorification of your name and image?

Stalin:

No, I do not.

Brown:

You mean all of the statues and monuments that are erected and all these places that are named after you are all done without your consent?

Stalin:

No. I consent, but if I did not, the people would be disappointed. The Soviet people love building statues to Stalin. It is their reaffirmation of the revolution. I admit, I do not like it, but I cannot stop them, any more than I can stop time.

Brown:
I see, how interesting. Um, a couple of days ago I was invited into an ordinary Soviet home. Your picture was on the wall of every room. And there was even a bust of you in the bathroom.

Stalin:
Is that so?

Brown:
Yes, I think Americans would find that amazing.

Stalin:
It's amazing to me. Our people have come a long way, but we have very far yet to go. We communists live for our visions.

Brown:
I see. Tell me, Uncle Joe, that brings up the coming visit of Mao Tse-tung. What are you going to tell him?

Stalin:
I'm not going to tell him anything. I'm just going to listen to him. After all, he will be my guest.

Brown:
They say he's a character, that Mao. What do you know about him, really?

Stalin:

All I know is that Mao is a great communist leader. That's all I need to know.

Brown:

There is a great deal of anticipation all over the world about this meeting.

Stalin:

There should be, this is a historic meeting. We look forward to concrete results.

Brown:

They say he is coming to borrow money.

Stalin:

Let the world say what it wants, what Mao himself says is all I care about.

Brown:

Again, very well put, Uncle Joe. May I tell you a joke, Comrade Stalin, with all due respect?

Stalin:

You may. What did they do, tell you we communists don't have a sense of humor? *(Stalin enjoys a hearty laugh.)*

Brown:

Good. Karl Marx comes back to earth. He asks his guardian angel where he shall live.

"Germany?" he says? "No," replies the guardian angel, "there are many fine Marxists there, but now it is divided and is not a very nice place to live." Then Marx says, "America, I'll move to America." "No," says the guardian angel, "there are many good and loyal Marxists in America, but it is capitalist and therefore not a very nice place to live." "Then," says Marx, "I'll live in Russia!" The guardian angel replies, "Russia is a very nice place to live, Karl, but there aren't any Marxists there at all." *(Brown laughs and looks at Stalin, who is still and calm.)*

Stalin:

You're a very brave man, Mr. Brown. Not everyone would dare tell the leader of the International Proletariat such a joke.

Brown:

I beg your pardon if I offended you, Comrade Stalin.

Stalin:

Just be careful what you say, Mr. Brown. Our Comrade Beria is a very resourceful and, I might add, ruthless operator. Don't you know you are followed everywhere, that your phone is tapped and that all your reports are intercepted by us before they reach your curious readers? Isn't that right, Comrade Proskrebyshev?

Proskrebyshev:

Perfectly right, Josef Vissarionovich.

Stalin:

So be careful what you say, Brown. Beria might take offense.

Brown:

Thanks for the advice, Uncle Joe. But I've got nothing to hide.

Stalin:

(Angrily.) Neither did Shoposhnikov, but we uncovered his villainy, right Proskrebyshev?

Proskrebyshev:

Absolutely right, Josef Vissarionovich.

Stalin:

But just to show you Comrade Stalin carries no hard feelings, I have a gift I want to present to you. Proskrebyshev! *(Stalin points to his boots and raises his leg. Proskrebyshev approaches him and pulls both his boots off.)* These are for you, Yankee, a finer gift I cannot give. Yes, you will return to the West with Comrade Stalin's boots.

Brown:

Why thank you. I'll never forget you, Uncle Joe.

Several knocks are heard at the door and Beria ENTERS.

Stalin:

Ah, Beria, you know Mr. Brown.

Brown:

I don't think we have been introduced.

Beria:

Well, not formally. *(Beria and Stalin laugh.)* How do you do?

Brown:

Look, Comrade Stalin has given me his boots.

Stalin:

Okay, that's it, time's up. Comrade Proskrebyshev, escort Mr. Brown downstairs.

Proskrebyshev:

Yes, Josef Vissarionovich. This way Mr. Brown.

Brown:

Goodbye. *(Shaking their hands.)*

Stalin:

Goodbye, goodbye Yankee.

Proskrebyshev and Brown EXIT.

Beria:

You gave him your boots? He'll make a million dollars on them!

Stalin:

Let him, he's a brave man. *(Pause.)* Beria, why don't we teach shorthand in our schools?

Beria:

I don't know, Josef Vissarionovich.

Stalin:

But you must know, Beria! *(Shouting.)* I want to know why a proper curriculum in the shorthand method of writing has not been developed by our Ministry of Education. If you find it is the result of a deliberate plot, then cut their heads off!

Beria:

At once, Josef Vissarionovich, Bitano.

Stalin:

Beria, *(handing him the shampoo and bath oil bottles)* here, send these to my daughter, Svetlana. You know how she loves Western goods.

Beria:

No, Josef Vissarionovich, she hates Western products.

Stalin:

Shut up and take them. And Beria…, Brown visited an apartment where a bust of Comrade Stalin is displayed in the bathroom. Find it and get rid of it. And further, discipline the family. *(Pause.)* No, never mind, thank the family for their adoration of the leader, give them ten rubles for the bust and take it with you. Then, donate the bust to the state historical museum in the family's name.

Beria:

Yes, Josef Vissarionovich.

Stalin:

And Beria, don't let it happen again. That's all!

Beria:

No, never again. Good day, Josef Vissarionovich.

Beria EXITS.

Stalin:

(To audience) Kind people, what's a leader to do? The people say they love Comrade Stalin, but they are confused. They love this nation, not me. They love the idea of devotion to the common good. I understand. I accept this

role they have given me. They people need a leader, therefore, I must dominate, for I trust my judgement better than any other. All over the world, people are weak. In my country, not only are we weak, but we are dumb and often we are hungry. We are also tired and frightened. In such circumstances, must not one man lead? Should not one man inspire the masses? You who know your history, know that it is true. Oliver Cromwell, Peter the Great Napoleon Bonaparte and even that rat Hitler.

Lights go down.

End of Scene Two

ACT ONE
Scene Three

SCENE: The Conference Room

TIME: An afternoon

AT RISE: A group of men (The Politburo) are all seated at a conference table, chatting. They are Beria, Molotov, Khruschev, Vorishilov, Malenkov and Mikoyan. Stalin ENTERS and they suddenly rise and become silent.

Stalin:
Please remain seated, Comrades. Greetings to you all. Beria, you are invited to dinner tonight.

Beria:
Thank you, Bitano.

Stalin:
And knock off the "Bitano" business.

Beria:
Yes, Josef Vissarionovich, forgive me.

Stalin:
Gentlemen, we have one item on today's agenda. Can you guess what it is? *(Stalin circles*

his extended arm in the air, then suddenly points at N.S. Khruschev.) Khruschev, you!

Khruschev:
Um, um, agriculture?

Stalin:
No, you idiot, not agriculture. You Vorishilov, do you know?

Vorishilov:
The defense of the country?

Stalin:
No, no, no, not the defense of the country. We have atomic weapons, that's history, Kliment. Mikoyan, do you know?

Mikoyan:
No, Josef Vissarionovich. Nobody can now what is in your head. You astound us all.

Stalin:
It's true. Well then, I'll tell you. Basketball, gentlemen. We're going to talk about basketball. *(Stalin then glares at Molotov.)* To some of you it is merely a sport, but to me, it is everything. Don't underestimate the things in this world that have political significance, right Georgi?

Malenkov:

Correct Comrade, exactly correct. We must see the political light of every shadow. This you have taught us again and again. That there is politics in everything. Why just yesterday...

Stalin:

Shut up, you idiot, of course there is politics in everything. But particularly in basketball. *(To Molotov)* I repeat, particularly in basketball. Comrade Foreign Minister, you are in charge of sports and athletic training. How can it be that the Soviet National Team has lost to the French in the European semi-finals? How can this be?

Molotov:

(Straining for words) It's my fault, Comrade Stalin. It's all my fault.

Stalin:

What a convenient formula you use to escape failure. But it will not work. Tell your comrades precisely why our team lost to a bunch of Parisian faggots.

Molotov:

Well, Comrade Stalin, this, after all was only our first year in the league. Our players are still not used to international competition. And we encountered French players who were taller than we expected.

Stalin:

Do you hear him, gentlemen? Molotov picked a bunch of shorties to play on our team. *(Shouting)* Two hundred million people in this country and you picked nothing but shorties. What am I to do with you, Molotov?

Molotov:

It's true Comrade Stalin, I have failed you. I shall resign my posts at once.

Stalin:

You're an ass, Molotov! Tell your comrades that you are an ass.

Molotov:

Comrades, I am an ass.

Stalin:

That's right, Molotov. Don't forget it. Due to your failings at the Foreign Ministry, our team was not well prepared and coached. Accordingly, you have brought shame and dishonor to your country, your people and your Party. *(By the end of this line, Stalin is fuming with anger.)*

All are silent.

Stalin pauses, calms himself down and continues.

In a few days, gentlemen, Mao Tse-tung will visit the Motherland. One of the agreements we will sign will be an athletic exchange pact to establish competitions between the best athletes in our two countries. Can you imagine if our team, the products of a generation of socialist prodding, should lose to the peasant Chinese? Mao's head would become as big as his belly!

Beria:

With all due respect, Josef Vissarionovich, on the whole, I think our teams have done remarkably well. At last year's Olympics, our athletes proved that they are among the best in the world.

Stalin:

They must be the very best, comrades, after all, the challenge to the human body mirrors the challenge to the human mind. In both these spheres, sound socialist principles must prevail. Socialist reasoning, as well as socialist athletic training, will win out. Is that clearly understood?

All clap and nod in agreement.

Let us summarize, gentlemen. This being their first year, I propose we reprimand Comrade Molotov and note this matter in his file. Poor man, he is overworked. Don't let it happen again, Comrade! *(Angrily)* Second, I want the team reorganized and a penalty shall be inflicted on all the coaches and players. Their salaries should be lowered and their standards should be raised. From now on they'll practice seven days a week. Furthermore, and you see *(Shouting)* to this Beria, I want a thorough evaluation of any ideological deviation that may have caused their loss. Is that understood, gentlemen?

All nod in agreement.

Very good, that's it. Beria you may return at 10 p.m. The others will go. Good day comrades.

All:

Good night Comrade Stalin.

All EXIT but Stalin.

Stalin:

(To the audience) What a bunch of little kittens they are. What will happen after I'm gone? I can't bear to think of it. Why me, why me?

Stalin shudders. Lights dim. The members of the Politburo, except Beria REENTERS, marching and line up across the front of the stage. They continue marching in place, then suddenly stop and say in unison:

> In darkest night, cold and clear
>
> The earth turns its sleeping head.
>
> Widows and children shiver in fright,
>
> Seeking refuge beneath the marital bed.
>
> Dusk to dawn, uncertain hours
>
> Have ever been the pleasure of evil minds
>
> No church bells toll anymore
>
> Only a single spotlight shines
>
> And who is caught in that beam
>
> We called friend just yesterday
>
> Nothing changed that we could see
>
> Except that chains he wears today.
>
> But soon the sun will shine
>
> And restore the light of man's desire.
>
> Soon the ground will ignite
>
> And burn us all in eternal fire.
>
> When, from the ashes others rise
>
> As others always must

The deeds of the past will never die
Nor memories turn to dust.

Lights go out. ALL EXIT.

End of Scene Three

ACT 1
Scene Four

SCENE: Stalin's Parlor

TIME: Late evening

AT RISE: Stalin is sitting alone in low lighting. He removes a framed photograph of a dark young woman from beneath his sofa. He looks at it for a long while. He moves and shifts it around in the light to view it from different angles. He then places it in his lap, face down and strengthens his expression. Lights come up and Rodianovna, his housekeeper and cook, ENTERS to set the table for dinner for three. Stalin quickly hides the photograph beneath a pillow and grabs and begins reading a copy of *Pravda* newspaper.

Stalin:

Eh, Rodianovna, stop making so much noise!

Rodianovna:

Josef, please. I must finish my work or dinner will not be ready in time. We are short-handed, you know. Beria removed the new house worker from Novgorod.

Stalin:

There is no figuring Beria. One day, he'll have all our heads.

Rodianovna:

If you permit me, Josef, I have a question I've always wanted to ask you.

Stalin:

(He returns to his reading and then exclaims:) Rubbish, they've named another factory after my daughter, Svetlana. Huh. As if it's not enough, every fictional Soviet heroine is named Svetlana. There are fashions named Svetlana and schools named Svetlana. What toads these people are. Rodianovna, the Soviet people, especially you Russians, are toads.

Rodianovna:

And you Georgians, what are you?

Stalin:

We are farmers and gossipers. Some of us are even leaders.

Rodianovna:

It is true, Josef, that Comrade Stalin is not really the son of a shoemaker from Gori, but from a line of princes? Is it true?

Stalin:

Who knows, Rodi? I may be the son of princes or the son of proletarians. What does it matter, I am Stalin now?

Rodianovna:

(Pause) May I ask who's coming to dinner tonight?

Stalin:

Beria and guess who?

Rodianovna:

Please do not interrogate me, Josef. Who could ever guess a question like that? You have more dinner guests than any Czar and they stay later, drink more and talk longer than I care to admit.

Stalin:

Then it'll be a surprise!

Rodianovna:

Forgive me, Josef, once again. Why do you hide that photograph? Why don't you keep it on the table next to you?

Stalin:

What photograph?

Rodianovna:

The photograph of your wife underneath your seat.

Stalin:

There is no photograph beneath my seat. You're crazy.

Rodianovna:

Yes, I've seen it a hundred times, you hide it there, why?

Stalin raises the newspaper covering his face as if to ignore her. Rodianovna approaches him, kneels down and reaches beneath the sofa feeling for the photograph. He then moves the paper just enough so that his eyes are revealed glaring coldly at her.

Rodianovna:

Forgive me, Josef, I must have been mistaken. I'll see to the food.

She quickly EXITS.

Stalin uncovers the photograph and once again stares at it, then returns it to its original hiding place beneath the sofa. He resumes his reading. Beria and Gelovani ENTER. Gelovani is dressed formally, resembling Stalin.

Stalin:

(Standing) Ah, Beria and who's this? Why it's Comrade Stalin. How are you?

Beria:

Good old Josef Vissarionovich. Allow me to introduce to you the magnificent actor, Gelovani.

Gelovani:

It is a pleasure, Josef Vissarionovich. I'm so happy to be here with you.

Stalin:

Good. Come sit down. Well, Gelovani, let's see how you look. *(Stalin circles and inspects Gelovani.)* Not bad, not bad. Your walk, let me see your walk.

Gelovani walks several steps.

Not so stiff, not so stiff. And remember, keep your left arm bent at the elbow. And always keep your head held high, like this. It's a sign of a noble nature. You must always remember that Comrade Stalin had a noble nature.

Beria:

It's enough to make you wince, Bitano.

Stalin:

What are you babbling about, Beria?

Beria:

No, nothing. I was just complimenting Comrade Gelovani on his fine and patriotic resemblance of you.

Stalin:

Yes, compared to all those half-baked Lenin look-a-likes, he's very good.

Gelovani:

Thank you, Josef Vissarionovich. I want to please you.

Stalin:

And the Soviet people?

Gelovani:

Of course Comrade, and the Soviet people.

Stalin:

And...

Gelovani:

(Stammering) Ah...Ah...Ah...

Beria:

And all the progressive, forward looking humanity.

Stalin:
Yes, Beria, very good.

Beria:
Thank you, Bitano.

Stalin:
All right, Comrade Gelovani. Permit me to say a few words before we dine. I will begin by noting that a serious burden falls on you. One could even say, an extremely serious burden. The Soviet peoples—indeed the peoples of all the world—are counting on you to show them what Stalin is really like. It is your duty, Comrade Gelovani, to show them what they have a right to know: The truth about Comrade Stalin. After all, we must not leave everything to the imagination in socialist theatre productions.

Beria:
(To himself) Oh brother.

Stalin:
What was that, Beria?

Beria:
Nothing Comrade Stalin, I didn't say a thing.

Stalin:

(Continuing) I was saying...it is your duty Comrade, to show them Stalin as he really is. The image you create must be an authentic image of their leader, established in an artistic mode and a stylistic form consistent with the revolutionary expectations of the masses. Remember Comrade, it is a titan of thought, a great philosopher and a historical leader that you are portraying on stage. The fact that it is me we are talking about is, of course, of no consequence.

Beria:

Such modesty! Eh, Gelovani, you must also remember to capture the leader's unyielding humility.

Stalin:

Now that you understand what is expected of you, Gelovani, I'll sleep easier knowing that the masses will be exposed to the true image of Stalin.

Gelovani:

Thank you for these special instructions, Comrade. I will always remember what you have told me.

Stalin:

You better! Now, gentlemen, to dinner. Comrade Gelovani, you sit here and Beria, you sit here. You see Gelovani, the Western bourgeoisie press always writes that Beria is to the right of Stalin. So I got used to that idea.

Stalin pours them each a glass of wine.

A toast, gentlemen, long live Stalin.

Beria and Gelovani:

Long live Stalin.

They all drink and laugh.

Stalin:

Thank you, Comrades. I can assure you that it is most gratifying to be appreciated by such fine communists as Stalin and Beria.

They all laugh.

Are there any questions you'd like to ask me, Gelovani?

Gelovani:

Um…, not that I can think of, Comrade.

Stalin:

Oh.

Beria:

(Breaking the pause) Bitano, Comrade Gelovani has informed me that he will be performing for the Chinese delegation when they arrive next week. *(To Gelovani)* Tell Comrade Stalin what you'll be performing.

Gelovani:

Hamlet.

Stalin and Beria:

(Both are startled; they exclaim) Hamlet?

Gelovani:

Did I say Hamlet? Forgive me comrades, I was not thinking. We will be presenting a new adaptation of the Chinese classic, *European Go Home*.

Stalin:

What? Has this been approved?

Gelovani:

Yes, Comrade Stalin, by Zhandov himself.

Stalin:

But Beria, we are Europeans ourselves, even us Georgians. We claim a European heritage.

Beria:

Might not Mao be offended, Bitano?

Stalin:

Or worse yet, he might think we're insulting him. We cannot afford any misunderstandings. Review the matter yourself. No, do it with Malenkov, he is a reliable judge of these things. If Georgi doesn't see anything wrong with it, then neither do I.

Beria:

Yes, Bitano. We'll get to it first thing in the morning.

Gelovani:

I really don't think that's necessary...

Stalin:

(To Beria) And make sure you look at it from Mao's point of view, Beria. He has an intellect of top caliber. His sense of insight is virtually unequalled. From everything I've heard about Mao, he is a leader to reckon with. They say he's keen and direct. I look forward to meeting him one on one. But in the meantime, I don't want any screw-ups over this adaptation, got it?

Beria:

Of course, Bitano. Don't worry, I'll take care of it along with Malenkov.

Stalin:

(To Gelovani) What is on your mind, comrade? Tell us, especially our gestapo…, *(pointing to Beria)* what you members of the Soviet intelligentsia are up to?

Gelovani:

I can only speak for myself, Josef Vissarionovich.

Stalin:

Well…?

Gelovani:

Hamlet, Josef Vissarionovich. I have been studying Shakespeare's *Hamlet*. It is truly a remarkable play.

Stalin:

And…?

Gelovani:

Well, we were thinking of a…ah…ah… requesting the Ministry of Culture Theatre Department for permission to stage the play. I am told that there is a good chance that Shakespeare will be permitted again in the Soviet Union. You're a scholar, Josef Vissarionovich, what do you think of *Hamlet*?

Stalin:

Well, of course, I am not a Shakespearean scholar. And as to whether you should produce this play in Moscow, well that's not for me to say. We have our critics and our ideological reviewers for that. More than that, I cannot say.

Gelovani:

Oh Comrade, *Hamlet* celebrates the sacred ideal of self-sacrifice. It is a beautiful play. Please tell me what you think?

Stalin:

Oh, I don't know, really. I haven't given Shakespeare much thought lately. *(Pause)* Well, if you really want my opinion Gelovani, and mind you, I don't wish to impose my ideas on creative people. *(Beria laughs suddenly. Stalin glares at him in return.)* In my opinion, *(To Beria)* humble as it is: *(To Gelovani)* To the extent I understand Shakespeare, I see Hamlet as a product of petit-bourgeois imagination. You see, the idea of abstract honesty and absolute spiritual chastity are foreign to the Soviet man. What can he learn from *Hamlet*? Reflection? Moral courage? No. Accordingly, I do not think it is wise for you to waste your enormous talents and our money for that medieval manifesto on individualism.

Gelovani:

(Stunned) I see.

Stalin:

But again, I must advise you, I do not wish to impose my views on such things. I make enough decisions around here. I'd prefer to leave decisions of this kind to the proper authority. *(He points to Beria.)* Like the KGB. *(He bursts out laughing.)*

Gelovani:

Yes, I see.

Beria:

Thank you for your expression of confidence, Josef Vissarionovich.

Rodianovna ENTERS with a cooking pot containing dinner. She places it on the dinner table, glances toward the three and suddenly shrieks.

Rodianovna:

Oh my God, two Comrade Stalins? *(She makes the Sign of the Cross.)*

Stalin:

Just leave it, we'll serve ourselves. *(Sharply)* Now good night!

She bows and EXITS.

Stalin:

These Russians, my friends, get more courageous with age. They are a strange race, very strange.

Beria:

So true, isn't that right, Comrade Gelovani?

Gelovani:

To tell you the truth, I feel sorry for them. We Georgians often forget how fortunate we are to have grown up in the bosom of the earth.

Beria:

Right you are Comrade Gelovani. Right you are!

Stalin:

Come, let's eat. Let's drink. I could eat an ox and drink a trough full.

They retire to the table. Lights go down. When they come up again, all three are drunk and babbling around the room.

Stalin:

Hey you, Comrade Minister of Police, did you investigate what happened to your hair? *(Laughs.)* You're all a bunch of little police captains. Where's your whistle? Blow your whistle.

All laugh.

Beria:
Tell me, Gelovani. Will you stage *Hamlet* and risk arrest?

Gelovani:
I play Stalin every day. What could be riskier?

All laugh.

Beria:
Tell me, Gelovani, when Comrade Stalin dies, what will you do?

Stalin:
(Wobbling) Anxious? Stop your plotting, Beria.

Beria:
For example, what if the body of the leader cannot take embalming? You don't think that's really Lenin in the mausoleum, do you?

Gelovani:
(Freezes) Huh?

Beria and Stalin laugh wildly.

Stalin:

Comrades, I propose a toast. To the great Soviet ah...ah...to the Soviet ah...eh, screw. Yes, to the great, most-great, most very great Soviet screw. We in our lifetimes are nothing, the screw will live on. Therefore, the Soviet screw is our brother.

Beria:

...and our sister.

Stalin:

A representation of the common man. The worker, the farmer and the peasant alike. All Hail to Soviet screws.

Gelovani and Beria:

All Hail!

They drink up.

Rodianovna ENTERS.

Rodianovna:

Oh my God!

Stalin:

Screws are not like nails, gentlemen. No they are more, much more and based upon the Marxist principle of the spiral theory. Yes, yes, the spiral. The further you turn a screw, the stronger it becomes. Comrade, I rededicate our country's thanks to the screw. Our nice, honest, deeply patriotic and sincerely devoted Soviet screw.

Gelovani and Beria:

Dasgrovia!

They all drink up and one by one fall onto the sofas and blackout.

Rodianovna walks up to them and looks at each of them and then at the table. She then pours herself a drink and says to the audience:

Rodianovna:

Who could ever have imagined it? The earth goes round and here is the leader, sleeping like a baby, oblivious to everything but the vodka in his blood.

She pours herself another drink.

His blood? Where did it come from? Sometimes I think from the serpents. Other times, I think from the white bear. *(Looking at Stalin)* I just don't know.

She tiptoes over to the sofa where Stalin is laying. She carefully kneels down and reaches beneath it. She pulls out the photograph and looks at it.

Such a beautiful young woman, no wonder he was so in love.

She then places it on the table next to the prostrate Stalin.

And he didn't even go to her funeral.

She EXITS.

Lights go down.

End of Act 1

ACT II

Scene One

SCENE: Stalin's Parlor

TIME: An afternoon

AT RISE: Sergo, a tired looking man in his 60s is sitting down, looking around with curiosity. He sighs regularly as if very tired. Sopha, his wife, who he has not seen for twelve years, ENTERS. They look at each other, freeze and then embrace.

Sergo:
Sopha, my dear Sopha. Is it really you?

Sopha:
Yes, Sergo darling, let me look at you. Handsome as ever!

Sergo:
Sopha, I knew I would see you again. I just knew it. And tell me, how is our dear Maika? Well, I hope?

Sopha:
I don't know. After you were arrested, they took our daughter away from me. I cried and begged, but they gave me no reasons. I was

kept all alone for two weeks and then they accused me of being an enemy of the people. Sergo, I was in exile too. I thought that surely you were dead.

She sobs.

Sergo:
No, dear Sopha. You mean you were also arrested? When?

Sopha:
Right after you. And those brutes took Maika from me and sent her to some orphans' asylum. I went crazy in there, Sergo. Crazy!

Sergo:
We're together and that's all that matters. Together again, at last. And this time forever. Don't worry, we will find our dear Maika. I promise you. And we'll be a happy family again. *(Freezing suddenly)* You haven't gotten remarried?

Sopha:
No, no… *(laughing)* How could I? They put me in a woman's camp working seven days a week sewing uniforms.

Sergo:
When were you released?

Sopha:
Just three weeks ago.

Sergo:
Oh, my poor Sopochka, let me see your hands. Oh, poor dear.

Sopha:
And you Sergo, when were you released?

Sergo:
Three days ago. They put me on a train with bodyguards, and escorted me straight here. I was blindfolded the whole time. Where are we anyway?

Sopha:
I don't know, they blindfolded me too. Maybe we're still not free?

Knocks are heard from the downstairs door. The couple, scared, embraces. Stalin ENTERS.

Sergo:
Josef Vissarionovich! You mean they got you too?

Stalin:
Sergo, Sopha, good to see you both again. Have you been treated well?

Sergo:

(Tenderly) Soso, is that really you?

Stalin:

(Embracing Sergo) It is, Sergo, my friend. You and your beautiful wife are both free as birds.

Sergo:

Soso, what is happening? Where are we?

Stalin:

Relax, Sergo. Everything is fine. You have your Sopha and your beautiful young daughter will be with you by evening. For the time being, you will be guests here at my house. I trust that answers your questions and meets with your approval?

Sergo:

It is too much, Soso. Why have you done this for us?

Stalin:

I'll tell you later. For now, just enjoy the company of your lovely Sopochka.

Stalin kisses her on the forehead.

Sopha:

How can we ever thank you, Soso? I thought everything was lost and here we are. And Maika will soon be here. Forgive me if I cry.

Sopha sits down and weeps.

Stalin:

Look at you, Sergo. You're a perfect advertisement for our Soviet correctional camps! You spent, what, twelve years in Siberia? And you are as pink as a suckling pig. And Sopha, fresh as a cucumber. Let me order some Georgian tea and cheese for you.

Stalin picks up a phone and says, demandingly:

Rodianovna, bring a pot of tea and some bread and cheese at once! Do we have coffee? No, okay, then bring tea!

Sergo:

Well, Soso, life in the camp was no picnic. But I knew it was a Soviet camp. We had a Party cell there. Just like the old days, eh Soso?

Stalin:

Of all my old Bolshevik Party comrades, Sergo, you were my favorite. Ah yes, those were the days. But they are gone, long gone. So are our old friends. They're all gone, too.

Sergo:

I don't understand, Soso. I know I missed the war, but were they all really killed by the fascist invaders?

Stalin:

Some were, but most got caught in the meat grinder in '37 and '38. You and me are the lucky ones.

Sergo:
What do you mean?

Stalin:

Our Minister of Police, Yezov, you remember that lunatic? He went nuts. Old Bolsheviks, proven revolutionaries were all cut down. Some of them, it's true, were Trotskyites, or Factionalists or Right Oppositionists, *(shouting)* and some Deviationists, and they deserved to die, but many good and honest Party regulars were innocently accused and condemned.

Sergo:

Tell me, Soso. What's become of our revolutionary friend, Georgi Starua?

Stalin:
Executed in '37.

Sergo:
How about the brave Gogo Benukidze?

Stalin:
He was executed in 38.

Sergo:
How about Lenin's favorite, Nikolai Voronov?

Stalin:
He was shot in 38 too.

Sergo:
And what about our comrade-in-arms, Sasha Makolevsky? Was he shot too?

Stalin:
No... *(Pause)* he was hanged.

Sopha:
Forgive me, Comrade Stalin. But may I ask why this has happened?

Stalin:
It got out of hand, poor woman. The problem of liquidating class enemies is not easily solved. Yes, there were excesses, but I think on a whole,

it was probably necessary to cleanse the Party before moving forward. A matter of dialectics, Comrade Sergo. But enough of this talk of the past. For you and your wife and daughter, there is only the future.

Stalin goes to a drawer and pulls out a document.

And here Comrade, allow me to present you with your new Party membership card and a Proclamation of the Supreme Soviet exonerating you and Sopha for your crimes.

Sopha and Sergo embrace each other.

And there's more. You will be given full compensation for the loss of your belongings. You will live in Moscow in an apartment from Comrade Stalin's personal quota.

Sergo:
Sopochka, it's too good to be true.

Stalin:
Don't interrupt me, Sergo. On Monday morning, you will report to Comrade Minister Molotov. Henceforth, you will be Deputy Minister of Foreign Affairs. You will receive a salary of $300 rubles a month, plus a car, a dacha in Sochi, and Sergo, permission to travel abroad.

Sergo:

Why have you done this Soso? I mean, last week I was in rags in the gulag and next week, a Deputy Minister? Are you playing with me? My beloved Communist Party, my country, my honor, are not things to be toyed with.

Stalin:

Sergo, I am General Secretary of the Communist Party of the Soviet Union, therefore, your superior. I will not be addressed by my subordinates with disrespect!

Sergo:

Forgive me, Soso. I mean Comrade General Secretary. I just don't understand.

Stalin:

Sometimes I don't understand either.

Pause. Stalin sits and motions Sergo and Sopha to also be seated.

You and I go back a long way, eh Sergo?

Sergo:

Yes, Josef, but sometimes it seems like only yesterday.

Stalin:

Then I pity you, my friend. For me, it was all such a long time ago. Sometimes, I think that it was all in another lifetime. Those days in Tiflis* are more like a dream to me. A dream that has images which I cannot comprehend, not even now. *(Pause)* You ask why I brought you here. Well, I'll tell you. Lately, I've been having this dream that I'm back on the banks of the river Lhiakva. Everything is just how I remember it as a boy, except one thing. The river is running backwards.

* Tiflis is the pre-Revolutionary name for Tblisi, the capital city of Georgia.

Sergo:

Backwards?

Stalin:

Yes, backwards.

Sopha:

I'm sure it's nothing, Soso. You work too hard, look at you. You're pale and sad faced. You shouldn't concern yourself with the mystery of dreams. Remember Julius Caesar. Let him be an example, Soso, it is only fitting.

Stalin:

No, it's different. My mind is not clouded with superstition as you may believe. This is real to me.

Sergo:

But how does your dream concern us, Soso?

Sopha:

Yes, Soso, is that why you have brought us here and given us so much?

Stalin:

Listen to me, both of you. Sergo, I do this because I owe it to you.

Sergo:

You owe it to me? What do you mean?

Stalin:

Yes. Remember, dear Sergo, Tiflis in 1909? You and I were co-conspirators in a plot to rob the local armory?

Sergo:

How can I forget, I spent three years in jail as a result?

Stalin:

Exactly. Have you often wondered how it is we got caught?

Sergo:

Yes, Soso, and I still can't figure it out. Our plans were flawless.

Stalin:

You see, Sergo, there was an informant.

Sergo:

Ahh…a collaborator.

Stalin:

Yes. *(Pause)* and I am he.

Sergo:

What?

Stalin:

It was I who betrayed you and our other comrades, Sergo. I, your Comrade Stalin.

Sergo:

I can't believe my ears. Again, you're joking with us?

Stalin:

It's no joke. Sopha, I betrayed your husband to the Czar.

Sergo:

Comrade Stalin, a Ohranka informer? Impossible!

Stalin:

Nonetheless, it's true. That particular job was the only time I ever really betrayed my comrades. But that once was enough. Until now, I have always been miserable about this. Now, Comrade Stalin is happy and unburdened by past mistakes.

Sergo:

I refuse to believe this, Koba*. Dear Koba. Our man, Stalin, the man of steel, a member of the Czar's secret police? It's impossible, I can't believe it.

* Koba was Stalin's early nom de guerre.

Stalin:

You think I am a liar?

Sergo:

(Standing up) Yes.

Stalin:

Look at this daredevil. He's just returned from exile and yet he has the courage to call Comrade Stalin a liar.

Sergo:

To me, Comrade Stalin is an ideal. Like Lenin.

Stalin:

Do you really think Lenin lived without sin?

Sergo:

Lenin and Stalin are ideals to me. I live and die by them.

Stalin:

Good fellow. What a good fellow you are. It's good just to look at you. Here we have a real Bolshevik, an unyielding Leninist. A Stalinist extraordinaire.

Sergo:

Thank you, Soso.

Stalin:

But you, you still don't believe me?

Sergo:

No.

Stalin:

Very well. In that case, you will be sent back to the camps. Sopha too. Your Party membership will be revoked; your exoneration will be canceled. I see that it's all been a mistake. Now you will suffer for calling me a liar.

Stalin picks up the phone.

Sopha:
Soso, please...

Sergo:
I am willing, Koba. It was in labor camps that we first felt the bonds of brotherhood.

Sopha:
Sergo!

Sergo:
It was in labor camps that we first organized.

Stalin:
(Angrily) Who is we?

Sergo:
We Bolsheviks! Honest Communists!

Stalin:
Very well, I will not contradict you. Go back to your camp. Establish a Party cell and study Marx's "Kapital." I am not joking. Take your pick. Stay here in Moscow as I have described, or go back and rot.

Sergo:

I can't believe my ears.

Sopha:

Why do you torment us Soso?

Stalin:

(Angrily) Because you refuse to believe the real Comrade Stalin. Instead, you cling to a phony ideal. Your mind is polluted by the glory of revolution. It shields the terrible truths of what we've made of our lives! There are no heroes in this world, Sopha. No heroes! Nobody is larger than life. Not Lenin, not Stalin, not Sergo! Nobody! Do you understand?

Sergo:

(Weeping) Why do you take away this thing I live for?

Stalin:

Faith, huh! Do you believe me or not?

Pause. Sergo sits next to Sopha.

Answer now! Damn it!

Sergo:

Why do you torture me?

Stalin:

(Sternly) Yes or no?

Sergo:

(Softly) Yes, I believe you.

Stalin:

Louder!!!!

Sergo:

Yes, I believe you!

Stalin:

(Stalin's angry and cold voice immediately becomes friendly.) Good Sergo. You did the right thing. I'm happy. Otherwise, you would have seemed larger than life, like those characters in our books and plays. Always patriotic, without the slightest weakness. But we are all human, Sergo. We are all weak.

They pause in silence.

Sergo:

How will we live now, Soso? I feel weak.

Stalin:

You will live magnificently, like all our ministers and their deputies. Occasionally, I will invite you to dinner and we can reminisce about our revolutionary past. Now, both of you, go and wait for your daughter.

Shouting to door.

Proskrebyshev! Comrade Proskrebyshev!

Proskrebyshev ENTERS from study door.

Stalin:

Escort our new Deputy Minister of Foreign Affairs and his lovely wife downstairs.

Proskrebyshev:

The young lady has arrived, Josef Vissarionovich.

Sopha:

Maika is here?

Stalin:

Good. Goodbye Comrade Deputy Minister. Goodbye Comrade Minister's wife. Go see your daughter.

Sopha:

Thank you for your help, Soso, we'll never forget this.

Sergo:

(Quietly) Goodbye Koba.

Stalin:

Don't think of it, Sergo. Think only of the future. Goodbye.

Stalin salutes him, Sergo stares and salutes back lamely.

They EXIT with Proskrebyshev.

Stalin:

(To audience) Ah, people. You mean you didn't think I felt guilt or thought about guilt. I do, though I'm not a sentimentalist, it's true. But that doesn't mean I don't possess sentiment. All I do, all I ever did, was absolutely necessary. It's never easy, but it's necessary nevertheless. I pity the man who feels no guilt.

He sighs and sits on the sofa.

To the audience.

Do you pity the man who does?

He looks around impatiently. He shouts:

Rodianovna! Where's the tea?

He lies down on the sofa and gets comfortable.

Tonight, I'll dream of the Lhiakva. We'll see which way it flows now.

Lights go down.

End of Act 2, Scene One

ACT 2

Scene Two

SCENE: Stalin's Parlor

TIME: An evening

AT RISE: Stalin is sitting alone in his den, reading a screenplay for a new movie. He is pacing back and forth as he reads, gesturing, stopping, scratching his head. There are knocks at the door. Beria ENTERS.

Beria:
Good day, Bitano.

Stalin:
Hello, Beria. Listen to this new movie manuscript about me. Another one, can you believe it? Listen to what supposedly intelligent people write about Comrade Stalin. *(Reading)* "In the never ending fields of Russia, Stalin appeared…"

Beria:
Baloney, Josef Vissarionovich. They should have written, "In the never ending fields of Russia, our dear teacher, the great Stalin appeared."

Stalin:

Stop crawling Beria. Anyway, come and sit down. *(They seat themselves, then Stalin looks up at Beria.)* Well, tell me Beria. Is it true?

Beria:

There's no easy answer, Bitano. My specialists assure me that Comrade Moroz wears earlocks, but he himself maintains they are sideburns.

Stalin:

Huh. That means it's still not clear.

Beria:

Josef Vissarionovich, this is a very difficult question. After all, the Soviet Constitution does protect freedom of religion.

Stalin:

Huh. That's all I need, a Jewish relative. A Jew who wears earlocks. What will Mao think?

Beria:

It's very delicate, Bitano. After all, he is the administrative head of the Academy of Experimental Physiology.

Stalin:

Who, Mao?

Beria:
No, Bitano. Comrade Moroz.

Stalin:
It doesn't matter, all administrative heads are crooks, isn't that right?

Beria:
Most assuredly, Josef Vissarionovich. All administrative heads and even their deputies are, in fact, crooks.

Stalin:
Right. Now my daughter is going to have a crooked Jew with earlocks for a father-in-law. What luck!

Beria:
What should we do? Should we arrest them both?

Stalin:
Beria, all you want to do is arrest people. Svetlana is my angel. She is all I have left to remind me of Nadia. I cannot bear to break her heart, even at the expense of my own.

Beria:
Well said, Bitano.

Stalin:
No. We must try something else. We must be discreet, too!

They both start to think.

I'll bet he's a chess champion.

Beria:
Who, the father?

Stalin:
No, the son, Moroz the younger. What's his name, Georgi?

Beria:
Grigory.

Stalin:
Whatever.

Beria:
According to my information, Bitano, he does not play chess at all. However, they say he's very good at ping pong.

Stalin:
Ping pong? That's not a Jewish game. *(Beria shrugs.)* The young nowadays. They are breaking away from the traditions of their fathers.

Beria:

It's true, Bitano. Exactly as you say.

Stalin:

Is he a skirt-chaser?

Beria:

Apparently not. On the whole, he seems to be an honorable Soviet Jew.

Stalin:

A lot your specialists know. Comrade Stalin is the leader of the International Proletariat. Communists do not have religious relatives. Think of how this could affect our foreign relations. At the very least, you must admit, it's embarrassing.

Beria:

True. May I suggest that they live together instead?

Stalin:

No, she won't do it. She even wants to take his name. Imagine that, Svetlana Stalin wants to become Svetlana Morozovna. It's outrageous! Why are children always such a burden on their parents, Beria?

Beria:

It's true, Bitano.

Stalin:

My first son, Yacov, now he was never a problem. If he wasn't betrayed by the Germans—he'd be here with us today. And Vasily, that drunk son of mine. He's a real pain, even to you security people.

Beria:

Bitano, you know you should not compare sons. Don't be too harsh on Colonel Stalin. After all, it's not easy for him being the son of the leader.

Stalin:

He's the son of the Soviet people, nothing more. *(Pause. Then Stalin muses to himself.)* Oh Svetlana, I know you try to please me, like your mother before you. But it's not easy, I know.

Beria:

Don't depress yourself again, Bitano, please. In just two days Mao will be here and you'll need to be at your best.

Stalin:

How can I feel well if all my doctors are untrustworthy, Beria? I wish Akaki Tsirodze was alive.

He'd help me, even if he was a quack. At least he was honest.

Beria:

Yes, he was something. The medicine man, the mumbo jumbo artist. I remember him well. They say he lived to age 106 years old. We Georgians, Bitano, have the world's healthiest blood.

Stalin:

Yes, yes, keep your editorials to yourself. Thanks to him, I no longer suffer from constipation.

Beria:

What a relief!

Stalin:

I miss him, I think, because he smelled like my father.

Beria:

Yeah, and like mine, too.

Stalin:

(Suddenly jumps up) Beria, I just thought of something! Remember how our Kremlin colleagues refused to see him because of fear that he was a witch doctor?

Beria:

Right, all we had to do was award him a diploma from Moscow Medical College.

Stalin:

Exactly, once we called him Doctor Tsirodze, everything changed. The Central Committee honored him. He acquired a vast following.

Beria:

Yeah, he even took up a complete floor at the Kremlin Hospital.

Stalin:

Right, well here's my point. The mere fact that we called him a doctor changed him into a doctor in our eyes, despite the fact that he really was only a simple Georgian peasant.

Beria:

I don't follow you, Bitano.

Stalin:

Well, the point is Beria, if you call a table a chair, then to everybody, a table is a chair, even though it really still is only a table.

Beria:

(Scratches his head) Of course, Bitano.

Stalin:
Then that settles the problem. And no one had to get arrested, eh Beria.

Beria:
(Puzzled) What problem, Josef Vissarionovich?

Stalin:
Moroz, you fool. Grigory Moroz! From now on, Moroz will be Morozov. Svetlana will be Svetlana Morozovna, a perfectly good Russian name.

Beria:
Brilliant, Josef Vissarionovich. What a brilliant idea! Moroz becomes Morozov. So simple, so clever. I hand it to you, Josef Vissarionovich, you are a sharp one. Very, very sharp.

Stalin:
Svetlana Morozov, that's more like it…

Beria:
Of course, Bitano.

Stalin:
Well, see it to Beria. At once and don't let this leak out.

Beria:

Never fear, Lavrenti Pavlovovich will take care of everything.

Stalin:

No blood, Beria, okay? Goodbye.

Beria EXITS

Stalin picks up the script and repeats to himself:

"In the never ending fields of Russia, our dear teacher, the great Stalin, appeared."

He pencils in the change on the manuscript and continues reading and gesturing.

Lights go down.

End of Act 2, Scene Two

ACT 2

Scene Three

SCENE: Stalin's Parlor

TIME: An afternoon

AT RISE: Proskrebyshev enters and makes way for Beria, and Mao-Tse-tung and Comrade Lee, who are wearing customary Chinese communistic attire.

Beria:

Thank you, Comrade Proskrebyshev. Chairman Mao, Comrade Stalin will be with us shortly. HE is attending to urgent state business, no doubt.

Lee whispers the translation into Mao's ear.

I'm sorry it's cold outside. The Russian winters you know, grant us little relief.

Again, Lee translates into Mao's ear.

Mao:
Siao.

Lee:
Chairman Mao said that he is not afraid of snow and frost. Chairman Mao said that snow

and frost are like the shadows of the sun and waters, like the reflection of winter stars in a summer stream, like wood and fire consumed in a dance of love. Chairman Mao said that the four seasons are like the seasons of a human life, that is to say: birth, maturity, old age and death.

Beria:

Yes, of course. How interesting! Comrade Lee, tell Chairman Mao that Comrade Stalin has anticipated this historic meeting very much.

Lee again translates by whispering into Mao's ear.

Mao:

Ssaioo!

Lee:

Chairman Mao said that for his entire life, he has dreamed of meeting Comrade Stalin. For him, Stalin is like the sound of a horn with which the shepherd calls his flock, like a diamond, a teacher, like a mother, a friend, yes, Chairman Mao says Comrade Stalin is like a signpost at the crossroads.

Beria:

A signpost?

Lee:

Yes, Chairman Mao said that even though his doctors had forbidden him to fly, he flew to meet Comrade Stalin on a jet of Soviet production. To Chairman Mao, it felt like a ride on a mountain eagle, journeying to the red valley of world revolution and liberation.

Beria:

I see. Very well put, Comrade Lee. Now if you'll forgive me, I will escort Comrade Stalin here. Comrade Proskrebyshev will serve you tea.

Beria EXITS. Lights go down.

Beria and Stalin appear at corner of upstage left under a spotlight.

Beria:

Josef Vissarionovich, Bitano. I must warn you. This Mao is a bizarre character. He's a poet or something. He talks in images, hazy images. I think he is suspicious.

Stalin:

Suspicious?

Beria:

Yes, him and his interpreter, Lee. If you could call that…an interpreter? …But it's my duty to advise you that we were not able to search his pockets. He brought 140 bodyguards with him. He's like a queen bee. A shoot out almost occurred between our guards and his.

Stalin:

Beria, you are an idiot. How dare you search Mao Tse-tung's pockets. How can you account for yourself?

Beria:

But Josef Vissarionovich, regulations.

Stalin:

To hell with regulations, Beria. He has 800 million people in his pockets. Do you know what would happen to us if 800 million Chinese started marching north? Remember Beria, a lot rides on this meeting. Come on, let's not keep this queen waiting.

Lights go up. Stalin and Beria ENTER. Proskrebyshev silently takes notes of the exchange.

Beria:

Chairman Mao, allow me to present Comrade Stalin, General Secretary of the Central Committee of the Communist Party of the Soviet Union.

Stalin and Mao embrace, kiss each other on the cheeks and shake hands.

Stalin:

Mao, I'm glad you're here. I trust you find Moscow suitable?

Lee whispers to Mao.

Mao:

Siaaooo!

Lee:

Chairman Mao said he feels at home here in the cradle of progressive thought. Like a hen come home to roost, like beautiful ideas put into execution. Yes, Chairman Mao said that Moscow reminds him of the red poppy, that beautiful and soulful flower that symbolizes the humble nature of world revolution.

Stalin:

Ah, the red poppy.

Lee:

Yes, Chairman Mao said that the image of the red poppy emerges from the velvet ocean at sunset, a bird of paradise, the glowing reflection of fear and joy, the peace and freedom of the Himalayas.

Stalin:

Yes, yes, of course, we understand Comrade Lee. Tell Chairman Mao I agree with him completely.

Lee whispers into Mao's ear. Mao nods with approval.

Lee:

(Continuing) Please forgive me Comrade Stalin. Chairman Mao said that the red poppy is the soul of the Japanese miner, the heart of the Filipino weaver, the conscience of the Indonesian fisherman; that it is a summons to the wind to be carried throughout the world. Chairman Mao said the red poppy will rush like a river to wash away the fields of poverty and oppression, like a child's teardrop falling to redeem the five-thousand-year-old wounds of the poor. In short, Chairman Mao said that Comrade Stalin is like the red poppy.

Stalin:

That's…ah, very charming Mao. Forgive me gentlemen if I confer with our Comrade Minister in Georgian, our native tongue.

Lee translates. Mao nods.

(To Beria) You're right, Beria. He's an idiot. A real marvel.

(Turning to Lee) Excellent, Comrade Lee.

(To Beria) I think I'd rather be *(Stalin turns and smiles at Mao.)* called a gangster than a red poppy, eh Beria?

(To Lee) Tell Chairman Mao that I am humbled before his visions.

Lee translates.

Mao:
Siiaooo!

Lee:
Chairman Mao said that...

Stalin:
Yes, yes, we know the mountain eagle and the wind...and all that kind of thing. We understand completely. *(To Beria)* Let's shut this Mandarin up. They say he likes gifts. Where are our gifts? Comrade Proskrebyshev, where are the Soviet people's gifts to Chairman Mao.

Proskrebyshev hands Stalin two boxes.

Ah, yes. Comrade Lee. On behalf of the Soviet people, I present Chairman Mao and the Chinese masses these recordings, in Chinese, of all my major speeches and writings. I hope you will find them useful.

Lee whispers to Mao.

Mao:

Siaaoo!

Lee:

Chairman Mao said he thanks Comrade Stalin very much. Chairman Mao has a gift for Comrade Stalin too.

Lee reaches into his case and pulls out a fan.

This ornamental fan is no ordinary fan. For on it spans the entire bibliography and text of Chairman Mao's writings and teachings to the Chinese people. Chairman Mao hopes that they will be of use to the Soviet masses.

Stalin:

(To Beria) Ah, a clever one we have here, Beria, how very clever. *(Looking at the fan)* Amazing, how do they write so small?

Beria:

They have small hands, Bitano.

Stalin:

Hummm...tell Chairman Mao we are very grateful and that we shall treasure this gift always. Now we have another gift we'd like to present to Chairman Mao.

Proskrebyshev hands Stalin a traditional multicolored Cossack dance costume from the second box.

To Chairman Mao, on behalf of the Communist Party, all its organizations and workers from Brest in the west to Vladivostok in the east, this traditional costume, from the Transcaucasian region of our country, is most sincerely bestowed.

Lee again translates into Mao's ear.

Mao:
Siiaaoooooooooh!

Stalin:
(To Beria) I think he just climaxed.

Beria:
Laughs.

Lee:
Laughs, but quickly raises his hand to his mouth.

Stalin:
Ah, Comrade Lee, you speak Georgian, too. You are a very bright young man. Tell me son, have you been in the party long? Two or three years?

Lee:

Forgive me Comrade Stalin, I have been a party member for twenty-eight years.

Beria:

(To Stalin, whispering aside) You're right, Bitano, they are amazing.

Stalin:

Well…

Lee:

Don't worry Comrade Stalin, I will only translate that which you tell me to translate. In this way, we will not have any unfair advantage.

Stalin:

That's very good, Comrade Lee. Our thanks.

He glares at Beria.

Would Chairman Mao like to try it on?

Lee whispers to Mao, Mao nods and Lee helps him to slip into the costume.

Lee:

What Chairman Mao said was that he again thanks Comrade Stalin and the Leninist-Stalinist Party for their gracious gift. And, Chairman

Mao said he also has another gift for Comrade Stalin, from the Shanghai Party Committee Women's Auxiliary; a gift of rare silk.

Lee pulls out of his case a bright yellow Chinese peasant outfit with a matching cap and red sash.

Chairman Mao would like to present it to Comrade Stalin in their name.

Stalin:
Thank you. What a…colorful gift.

(Aside to Beria) This is more than coincidental, Beria. How could they know what we were planning to give him?

Beria:
He murmurs and shrugs.

Stalin:
You find out Beria, first thing tomorrow morning, you find out!

Beria:
Yes, Bitano. By tomorrow morning, we'll have the traitor.

Stalin:
(To Lee) Tell Chairman Mao that I am delighted.

Mao:
Siiaoooo!

Lee:
Chairman Mao said he thinks Comrade Stalin would like to try it on.

Stalin sneers at Beria.

Stalin:
(Sighs) Yes, of course, I would love to try it on.

Beria snickers off to the side as he assists Stalin to put the costume on.

Lee:
Chairman Mao is pleased at his meeting with Comrade Stalin and Minister Beria. He further wishes to thank the Soviet people and their party leaders for the hospitality…

Stalin:
(To Beria) Here we go again.

Lee:
(Continuing) …and for their generosity. Chairman Mao said that the exchange of gifts between you is like the exchange of two brother mountain lions over the prey they both have

captured, like a seafarer's sail, filled up by the wind, like a star, a net, a...

Stalin:

(Interrupting) Tell Chairman Mao that we agree wholeheartedly. *(To Beria)* Enough of this Beria. Poor Proskrebyshev can hardly keep up with this blabbermouth.

Lee:

And lastly, Chairman Mao said he is tired and wishes to rest before the state dinner tonight.

Stalin:

Really? Well, good. I'm tired too. Beria, issue a communique with Comrade Lee. Let the whole world know that Chairman Mao and Comrade Stalin are great friends and brothers in arms. Now leave us to rest. Tell the entire world that this afternoon. Chairman Mao and Comrade Stalin napped together in the same room, side by side.

Beria:

As you command, Josef Vissarionovich. Comrade Lee, please...

Beria, Lee and Proskrebyshev EXIT.

Mao:

Siiaooo

Stalin:

Good Mao, very good. *(Shows him to the couch.)* Lie down here and rest for a while. *(Mao does so quietly.)* Good, and I sleep right here.

Stalin lies down on the other couch. Mao starts to chant. Stalin gets up, stares at Mao, who is lying there with his eyes closed, droning on.

To audience

Who does that Communist think he is, God?

Stalin lays back down and covers his ears with pillows to escape the din coming from Mao.

Why me? Why me?

Lights go down.

End of Act 2, Scene Three

END OF PLAY

Epilogue

The following is a news item, reported by The Associated Press on Dec. 22, 1999:

It was Stalin's 120th birthday Tuesday, and Georgians and Russians loyal to the memory of the Soviet dictator gathered to celebrate.

In the Georgian town of Gori, about a thousand people, including women with scarves around their heads and medal-wearing war veterans, walked up to the 10-foot statue of Stalin outside the museum that encloses the house in which he was born in 1879.

Wreaths carpeted the square in front of the monument.

Josef Stalin died in 1953. He is believed to be responsible for the deaths of at least 20 million people.

About J. Ajlouny

Playwright J. Ajlouny is an attorney, agent, and writer from Detroit. His many plays include *The Trial of William Shakespeare*, *The Red Poppy: Josef Stalin at Home*, and *Marilyn, Norma Jean and Me*. He is also the author of more than a dozen humor and popular reference books under the pen name Joey West. Josef is director of The Federal Bureau of Entertainment, a production company that specializes in the development and presentation of solo theatre plays and musical reviews.

Fresh Ink Group
Independent Publisher

Imprint: Fresh Ink Group
Imprint: Push Pull Press

𝔻

Hardcovers
Softcovers
All Ebook Platforms
Worldwide Distribution

𝔻

Indie Author Services
Book Development, Editing, Proofing
Graphic/Cover Design
Video/Trailer Production
Website Creation
Social Media Management
Writing Contests
Writers' Blogs
Podcasts

𝔻

Authors
Editors
Artists
Experts
Professionals

𝔻

FreshInkGroup.com
Email: info@FreshInkGroup.com
Twitter: @FreshInkGroup
Google+: Fresh Ink Group
Facebook.com/FreshInkGroup
LinkedIn: Fresh Ink Group

ADVENTURES IN LENINLAND

Prior to the collapse of Communism and the break-up of the Eastern-bloc empire of the U.S.S.R., a humorist and fledgling Kremlinologist was invited to tour the vast Red Landscape. Along the rails and roads traveled, he met a cast of colorful characters and faced a host of bizarre situations that only such a world can produce. These stories and essays portray a few of the fascinating, tragic, and whimsical things he discovered.

Fresh Ink Group

Meet William Shakespeare

Much has been explored about Shakespeare and his life, but little is known about how this small-town boy with a grammar-school education came to pen masterworks like *Hamlet* and *King Lear*. In *Meet William Shakespeare*, playwright J. Ajlouny creates authentic and plausible explanations that answer centuries-old questions about the man and his work. The result is an educational and fun portrait of Shakespeare, as told by The Bard himself.

PUSH PULL PRESS / Fresh Ink Group

The Trial of William Shakespeare

Few men have endured the indignity of having their very existence challenged as thoroughly as William Shakespeare, late of Stratford-upon-Avon. From scholars to amateur enthusiasts, many cannot bring themselves to believe he wrote his own body of work. Playwright J. Ajlouny presents the arguments for and against, all statements and proofs drawn from the historical record. Everybody must decide for himself, but *The Trial of William Shakespeare* makes the controversy both intriguing and fun.

Push Pull Press/Fresh Ink Group

Marilyn, Norma Jean and Me

In this boisterous but sensitive drama, playwright J. Ajlouny looks beyond public image to find the heart of this young woman thrust wildly into fame as a sex symbol. Presented as a play-in-the-making within a play, *Marilyn, Norma Jean and Me* weaves biography with humor to explore the movie star's widely speculated desire to leave Hollywood for Broadway. The author imagines her innocence and vulnerability, her friendliness and loyalty, even as the public image threatens to steal her humanity. This play is a masterpiece, not just because it is so good, but for its powerful way of finding the real Norma Jean in the legend known as Marilyn Monroe.

PUSH PULL PRESS / Fresh Ink Group

WHO SAID THAT?

Who Said That? provides an entertaining and authoritative reference for the origins and meanings of our common figures of speech.

- Who said 100+ famous expressions?
- Who *really* said them?
- What did they actually say?
- What did they actually mean?
- Why did they say them that way?
- Who repeated what was said?

Surprisingly true, sometimes strange, always fascinating, the stories about whence came these expressions will entertain, educate, and even amaze you.

Fresh Ink Group

FIGURATIVELY SPEAKING

A figure of speech is an expression in which the words are used, but not in their literal sense, to create a more forceful or dramatic meaning. They are often in the form of metaphors, similes and hyperbole. "A fountain of knowledge," is a good example. "Stretching the truth," is another.

With Figuratively Speaking, we finally have a thesaurus to discover these phrases' origins and the sources of their meanings. Categories include:Attitudes, Body Types, Competition, Creature Comforts, Letting Loose, Ethics, Influence, Life-Health-Death, Money, Personal Space, Personality Types, Speech, Thinking Power, Time, Trouble-Turmoil-Commotion, and The World of Work. Whether reading it for fun, researching phrases you use, or studying the symbolic foundations of our language, Figuratively Speaking is the resource you'll reach for time and again.

Fresh Ink Group

www.ingramcontent.com/pod-product-compliance
Lightning Source LLC
Chambersburg PA
CBHW071513040426
42444CB00008B/1618